DAVID JEREMIAH

AIRSHIP GENESIS

LEGENDARY BIBLE ADVENTURE

™

DISCOVERY

UNDERSTANDING THE 66 BOOKS OF THE BIBLE FOR KIDS

CONTENTS

BOOKS OF THE NEW TESTAMENT

AIRSHIP GENESIS

LEGENDARY BIBLE ADVENTURE

THE GENESIS EXPLORATION SQUAD

Joules, Cameron, Rupert, Emma,
Gabi, Logan, and Wyatt

INTRODUCTION

Did you know that the Bible contains everything we need to know about living today and for eternity as well?

It contains the wisdom of God, and the mind of Christ, His beloved Son.

If you need to discover answers, the Bible has them!

It teaches us how to live, how to love others like God loves us, how to overcome our fears, how to share our faith, and how to fight against temptation Satan may put into our path.

The Bible is inspired—meaning that God inspired men to write it as the Spirit gave them the words.

The Bible is unique—there is no other book like it.

The Bible is necessary—we need to know it and understand it.

The Bible is complex—it contains 66 books written by more than 40 authors, but it is understandable if you study it.

Discovery: Understanding the 66 Books of the Bible for Kids is a way for you to better understand what each book in the Bible is about, why it was written, and what you should know about it.

It is our prayer that as you read this book, you will discover many blessings as you learn about God and His Word to us—the Bible.

BOOKS OF THE

OLD TESTAMENT

GENESIS

CHAPTERS
50

AUTHOR:
MOSES

KEY VERSE:

"In the beginning God created the heavens and the earth." Genesis 1:1

(Page 2 in the *Airship Genesis* Kids Study Bible)

Where did everything come from? When did it all begin? Who made the stars, trees, animals, and people? You'll find the answers to those questions in Genesis. This is the first book of the Bible, and it opens with the words: "In the beginning God created the heavens and the earth."

The first eleven chapters of Genesis are full of stories about ancient times. Here you'll see how Adam and Eve made some wrong choices that forever changed the world and how a great flood nearly destroyed everything.

In Genesis 12–50, we learn how God chose Abraham and his family to begin a new nation, Israel, which would one day bring a Savior named Jesus to the world.

Genesis, then, is the book of beginnings—and it's a good place to begin your exciting Bible adventure. In Genesis you will begin your discovery of God's Word and what it means to you!

PRAYER:

Dear Lord, help me to remember that You created
everything and that You have an amazing plan
for us that is found in Your Word.

EXODUS

CHAPTERS
40

AUTHOR:
MOSES

KEY VERSE:

"Do not be afraid. Stand still, and see the salvation of the Lord, which He will accomplish for you today." Exodus 14:13

(Page 82 in the *Airship Genesis* Kids Study Bible)

If you like tales of adventure, you'll love Exodus. It's filled with heroes who stood up to bullies, plagues with snakes and locusts, and a sea that split apart like a canyon. It tells how Moses, prince of Egypt, freed a group of slaves to become a great nation.

The first part of Exodus (chapters 1–24) describes what happened when Moses was a baby and floated in the River Nile in a basket. And how he grew up to become a leader who told Pharaoh: "Let my people go!" God redeemed (or freed) Israel from slavery, and you'll read about miracles He performed and the laws He gave. In chapter 20, you'll find the Ten Commandments.

The last part of the book (chapters 25–40) explains how Moses built a special tent called the tabernacle where the people of Israel could worship God.

When you read Exodus, remember—the same God who rescued Israel also redeems us so we can serve Him all our lives.

*To read the Ten Commandments in Exodus 20, go to pages 88-90 in the *Airship Genesis* Kids Study Bible.

PRAYER:

Dear Lord, whenever I am afraid, please remind me that You are with me and that You will rescue me when I am in trouble.

LEVITICUS

CHAPTERS
27

AUTHOR:
MOSES

KEY VERSE:

"I am the Lord your God ... and you shall be holy; for I am holy." Leviticus 11:44

(Page 125 in the *Airship Genesis* Kids Study Bible)

In Genesis, God chose Abraham and his family to become a great nation. In Exodus, Moses led that nation out of slavery, into the desert, and toward the land God had promised to give them as their home. In Leviticus, the Lord told them how important it was for them to be holy.

The word *Leviticus* comes from the word *Levi*. That was the name of the tribe of Israelites who served as priests. In the Old Testament, priests helped people to be holy. That's the great theme of Leviticus: being holy. That means living as God wants us to, being pure, obedient, and good. If you went through Leviticus and circled every time you saw the word *holy*, you would have 78 circles. The key verse is Leviticus 11:44: "I am the Lord your God ... and you shall be holy; for I am holy."

Leviticus teaches us to be careful in what we say, how we act, and where we go. We serve a holy God, and we want to please Him in every way.

PRAYER:

Dear Father, I ask for Your help in the choices I make each day—I want to be obedient and honor You with my life.

NUMBERS

CHAPTERS
36

AUTHOR:
MOSES

KEY VERSE:

"The Lord bless you and keep you; the Lord make His face shine upon you, and be gracious to you; the Lord lift up His countenance upon you, and give you peace." Numbers 6:24-26

(Page 155 in the *Airship Genesis* Kids Study Bible)

How many people are in your school? To know the answer, you would need to count each person: *One, two, three* .... That's what Moses did with Israel. He didn't know how many people had followed him out of Egypt, so he counted them. He counted them twice—once in chapter 1 and later in chapter 26. He especially counted those in Israel's army so he would know the number of his troops. That's why this book is called Numbers.

But Numbers is about more than counting people. It's about counting on God. That's something the Israelites failed to do. In Numbers 13 and 14, you'll read about spies who scouted the Promised Land. Two of the spies—Joshua and Caleb—trusted the Lord. The others discouraged the people from trusting God. As a result, the Israelites wandered around for about forty years like people lost in the desert.

Numbers teaches us we should count on God and His promises in every situation. He knows how to be our Guide and our Guard.

PRAYER:

Dear God, thank you for being my guard and guide in every situation I face in life.

DEUTERONOMY

CHAPTERS
34

AUTHOR:
MOSES

KEY VERSE:

"The eternal God is your refuge, and underneath are the everlasting arms."
Deuteronomy 33:27

(Page 231 in the *Airship Genesis* Kids Study Bible)

What do you think about as you fall asleep? When you wake up? According to Deuteronomy, we should often think about Bible verses. Deuteronomy 6:7 says, "Talk of them when you sit in your house, when you walk by the way, when you lie down, and when you rise up."

Deuteronomy is a long word, but it's a little like *duet* and *duo*. It means "two," or "second." As you read this book, imagine Moses as an old man, teaching his lessons a second time to the younger generation. Forty years earlier, he taught the older generation. Now here in Deuteronomy he teaches his truths a second time to those getting ready to enter the Promised Land. These are his last words in the Bible.

In Deuteronomy, you'll find lots of great verses to think about when you go to bed and when you get up. Here is a great verse to memorize: "The eternal God is your refuge, and underneath are the everlasting arms" (Deuteronomy 33:27).

PRAYER:

Dear God, thank you for Your promises and Your presence—You are there when I wake up and when I sleep—You are always with me.

JOSHUA

CHAPTERS
24

AUTHOR:
JOSHUA

KEY VERSE:

"As for me and my house, we will serve the Lord." Joshua 24:15

(Page 260 in the *Airship Genesis* Kids Study Bible)

Joshua is for explorers. It tells how a great general named Joshua became the leader of Israel after the death of Moses. He led them across the Jordan River to a city named Jericho, and they marched around this city until God caused the walls to tumble down. That allowed the Israelites to explore all the land above Jericho. They drove out the evil people living there and claimed the land God promised them.

The first part of the book (chapters 1–12) tells how Israel captured the Promised Land. The last part of the book (chapters 13–24) tells how they divided it up among their twelve tribes.

Joshua 1:9 says, "Have I not commanded you? Be strong and courageous. Do not be afraid; do not be discouraged, for the Lord your God will be with you wherever you go" (NIV). The book of Joshua shows us God has a plan for exploring life. When we decide to follow Him, He will be with us wherever we go.

PRAYER:

Dear God, I want to be courageous like Joshua so that others will learn about You from my example of faith.

JUDGES

CHAPTERS
21

**AUTHOR:
SAMUEL**

KEY VERSE:

"The Lord raised up judges who delivered them out of the hand of those who plundered them." Judges 2:16

(Page 265 in the *Airship Genesis* Kids Study Bible)

AIRSHIP GENESIS

LEGENDARY BIBLE ADVENTURE

Would you like to meet the strongest man on earth? How about a man who defeated an army with torches? Or a woman who won a battle and sang about it? These are some of the heroes you'll meet in Judges.

According to Judges 2:10, after Joshua died the Israelites forgot the Lord: "Another generation arose after them who did not know the Lord nor the work which He had done for Israel." The stories in Judges are sometimes sad, because sad things happen when we forget God. But you'll meet good people in this book too, like the leaders mentioned above—Samson, Gideon, and Deborah.

The first part of the book (chapters 1–16) describes these Judges. The last part of the book (chapters 17–21) tells grim stories about people who forgot the Lord.

We're never too young to love God and never too old to serve Him. If you begin now, you'll be glad you did. We don't want to be the generation who forgot to follow God.

PRAYER:

Dear God, thank You for being my strong defender—I want to follow You all the days of my life.

RUTH

CHAPTERS
4

**AUTHOR:
UNKNOWN**

KEY VERSE:

"Entreat me not to leave you, or to turn back from following after you; for wherever you go, I will go; and wherever you lodge, I will lodge; your people shall be my people, and your God, my God." Ruth 1:16

(Page 294 in the *Airship Genesis* Kids Study Bible)

When you hear about Bethlehem, perhaps you think of Christmas. But centuries before Jesus was born, something else happened in Bethlehem. A woman named Ruth met a landowner named Boaz, and their love story became one of the most famous in history.

Here's what happened. In the days of the judges, a famine struck Israel. One of Bethlehem's families moved away to find food. The mother's name was Naomi. After her husband and sons died, Naomi returned home. Her daughter-in-law, Ruth, went too. Ruth became a follower of the Lord.

One day Ruth went into the fields looking for grain. But God wanted to give her more than food. He wanted to give her a husband. The landowner saw her, and it was love at first sight. Their son, Obed, later became the grandfather of King David and an ancestor of Jesus.

The book of Ruth shows us God loves us whether we're rich or poor, and He knows how to provide all we need. That's what makes a great love story. It's the love of God!

PRAYER:

Dear Father, thank You for watching over me in every situation and providing for my needs, as You did for Naomi and Ruth.

1 SAMUEL

CHAPTERS
31

AUTHOR:
SAMUEL

AIRSHIP GENESIS
LEGENDARY BIBLE ADVENTURE

KEY VERSE:

"To obey is better than sacrifice."
1 Samuel 15:22

(Page 317 in the *Airship Genesis* Kids Study Bible)

Have you heard how the shepherd boy David defeated a giant with his slingshot? That's one of the adventures in 1 Samuel, but there are others. In this book you'll also read how the boy Samuel heard God speaking to him at night and how Saul became king of Israel but lost his life. Samuel, Saul, and David—those are the main characters in this book.

- We learn about Samuel in chapters 1–8. His mother, Hannah, dedicated him to the Lord when he was very small.

- Saul shows up in chapters 9–15. He was tall and handsome, but he made tragic mistakes.

- We meet David in chapter 16, and the rest of the book is mostly about his adventures.

The key thought is: "Man looks at the outward appearance, but the Lord looks at the heart" (1 Samuel 16:7). It's not what we look like on the outside that counts. The Lord sees what we're really like, and He wants us to obey Him with all our hearts.

PRAYER:

Dear Lord, as I face giants in my life, remind me it isn't my size or strength that is important—it is Your power that will protect me, for the battle belongs to You.

2 SAMUEL

CHAPTERS
24

AUTHOR:
NATHAN & GAD

KEY VERSE:

"The Lord lives! Blessed be my Rock!
Let God be exalted, the Rock of my
salvation!" 2 Samuel 22:47

(Page 364 in the *Airship Genesis* Kids Study Bible)

Ever wonder what it's like to be a king or queen? It's not just living in a castle or riding in a carriage. Second Samuel takes us inside the palace of King David and lets us see his successes, struggles, and sins.

The book opens with David learning of the death of King Saul in battle. In chapter 5, David replaced him as king and made Jerusalem his capital. The next chapters describe his victories in leading the armies of Israel.

Everything changed in 2 Samuel 11, when David disobeyed God. He confessed his mistake and God forgave him, but David faced many problems. Near the end of 2 Samuel is a song David wrote summing up his life. He said, "I called to the Lord, who is worthy of praise, and have been saved from my enemies" (2 Samuel 22:4, NIV).

You may never be a king or queen, but when you know Christ, you're the child of King Jesus. You can call to Him, who is worthy of praise, and He will help you.

PRAYER:

Dear God, I praise You! You are my King and
the Rock of my salvation.

1 KINGS

CHAPTERS
22

**AUTHOR:
POSSIBLY
JEREMIAH**

KEY VERSE:

"Keep the charge of the Lord your God: to walk in His ways, to keep His statutes, His commandments, His judgments, and His testimonies, as it is written in the Law of Moses, that you may prosper in all that you do and wherever you turn." 1 Kings 2:3

(Page 372 in the *Airship Genesis* Kids Study Bible)

If you wanted to dress up like Solomon, you'd put on the most colorful robe in the store, wrap a turban around your head, stuff your feet into fancy shoes, and wear a wise look on your face. Solomon was the wisest king who ever ruled, but he didn't always live like it. His story is in 1 Kings 1–11.

The rest of the book (chapters 12–22) describes the kings who came after him.

Along the way, you'll meet the prophet Elijah. He didn't wear fancy clothes, but he knew how to pray. When Elijah prayed, incredible things happened.

Dressing up is all right; but prayer is more important than clothes. If Solomon had worried less about putting on his shoes and more about walking with the Lord, he would have been a better king. The Bible says, "Elijah was a man with a nature like ours, and he prayed earnestly" (James 5:17).

Be like Elijah and you'll become truly wise.

PRAYER:

Dear Lord, help me to trust in Your wisdom—to pray like Elijah—and to choose right instead of wrong.

2 KINGS

CHAPTERS
25

AUTHOR:
POSSIBLY JEREMIAH

KEY VERSE:

"So he answered, 'Do not fear, for those who are with us are more than those who are with them.'"
2 Kings 6:16

(Page 413 in the *Airship Genesis* Kids Study Bible)

Reading 2 Kings is like watching a parade of people fall down, each knocking into the next until no one is standing. It's the story of the last kings of Judah and Israel, and most of them were failures. By the time we get to the last king, Zedekiah, the nation of Judah no longer existed. The Babylonian Empire defeated it.

We can learn from their mistakes. We can also learn by a few of the good people in this book, including a fearless prophet named Elisha—a miracle man.

After his teacher, Elijah, went to heaven in a chariot of fire, Elisha pressed on to do some wonderful things for the Lord. In 2 Kings you'll read how God used him to raise the dead, keep a pot of oil flowing, turn spoiled soup into a healthy lunch, and make an ax head float.

God needs people like Elisha in terrible times. He needs you. Even when everyone else seems to be falling and failing, God can help you stand up like Elisha. He can use you to proclaim His message.

PRAYER:

Dear Lord, help me to remember how You cared for Elisha during his life, and use me to share the message of Your love with those around me today.

1 CHRONICLES

CHAPTERS
29

AUTHOR: POSSIBLY EZRA

KEY VERSE:

"Oh, give thanks to the Lord! Call upon His name; make known His deeds among the peoples!" 1 Chronicles 16:8

(Page 455 in the *Airship Genesis* Kids Study Bible)

Who was your great-great-great-great-great grandfather? In the Bible, people were concerned about things like that. That's why the first nine chapters of 1 Chronicles are lists of the names of people who had been a part of the history of Israel. It's a long family tree.

By the time we get to chapter 10, we're ready for some action— and that's what we get. Chapters 10–29 are all about David. It's an exciting story—how David became king (chapters 10–12); how he brought the Ark of the Covenant to Jerusalem (chapters 13–17); how he won victories over his enemies (chapters 18–20); how he wanted to build a temple (chapters 21–27); and what happened at the end of his life (chapters 28–29).

First Chronicles wants us to know about God's promise to David that someone from his family would always be a king. That promise was fulfilled when Christ came from the line of David (see Matthew 1:1).

God is good at keeping His promises. He has kept every promise He ever made, and He will keep His promises to you.

PRAYER:

Dear Lord, I praise You for Your goodness and faithfulness
to Your people, including me!

2 CHRONICLES

CHAPTERS
36

AUTHOR:
POSSIBLY EZRA

KEY VERSE:

"If My people who are called by My name will humble themselves, and pray and seek My face, and turn from their wicked ways, then I will hear from heaven, and will forgive their sin and heal their land." 2 Chronicles 7:14

(Page 477 in the *Airship Genesis* Kids Study Bible)

If you've heard of the series of books called *The Chronicles of Narnia*, then you know the word *chronicles*. It means "history" or "story." Second Chronicles is the history of the nation of Israel from the days of Solomon until its capital of Jerusalem was destroyed. But even then, the Lord wasn't finished. The last chapter of the book tells how some faithful people began rebuilding their nation and their temple. They didn't give up.

One of the great themes of 2 Chronicles is the temple of God in Jerusalem. If you circle the word *temple* in 2 Chronicles, you'll find it occurs more than forty times. The temple was God's headquarters among His people in the Old Testament. The Babylonian Empire destroyed the temple in 2 Chronicles 36, but the story wasn't over. The book ends with a challenge to rebuild it.

In some ways, 2 Chronicles tells the same story as 1 and 2 Kings, but it's different. It shows us that God always wins in the end. He brings back His people. He doesn't give up on us—and He never wants us to give up on Him.

PRAYER:

Dear God, help me remember when trouble comes
to pray and keep my eyes on You!

EZRA

CHAPTERS
10

AUTHOR:
POSSIBLY EZRA

KEY VERSE:

"And they sang responsively, praising and giving thanks to the Lord: 'For He is good, for His mercy endures forever toward Israel.' Then all the people shouted with a great shout, when they praised the Lord, because the foundation of the house of the Lord was laid." Ezra 3:11

(Page 512 in the *Airship Genesis* Kids Study Bible)

Have you ever seen a house after it burned down? Sometimes it's nothing but a heap of ashes. Imagine clearing away the soot and rebuilding the house. That's what the people of Israel did in the book of Ezra. They wanted to rebuild their burned-down temple. It was hard work, and at first it didn't go well. But they didn't give up.

The book of Ezra has ten chapters. The first six tell how about 50,000 Jews returned to Jerusalem from refugee camps in Babylon and began rebuilding the temple. Their enemies tried to stop them. But finally the temple was rebuilt and the people celebrated.

The last part of the book (chapters 7–10) describes how a mighty Bible teacher named Ezra came to Jerusalem. He taught the nation of Israel to study the Word of God.

The book of Ezra teaches us to keep working. The Lord will do something wonderful before it's all over He can help people rebuild their lives.

PRAYER:

Dear God, when I am challenged to do something for You, please remind me to trust in Your plans as I do the work.

NEHEMIAH

CHAPTERS
13

AUTHOR:
NEHEMIAH

KEY VERSE:

"The joy of the Lord is your strength."
Nehemiah 8:10

(Page 531 in the *Airship Genesis* Kids Study Bible)

In the days of Nehemiah there were streets, stores, and houses. And there was a newly rebuilt temple. But something was missing. There was no wall around the city. In Bible times, cities needed walls to keep out invaders. Nehemiah was a leader who heard about the broken walls of Jerusalem. He led the construction project to repair the damage.

There are thirteen chapters in his book. Chapters 1–7 describe how the wall was rebuilt. In chapter 8, the citizens had a rally to study the Law of God. Chapters 9–13 explain how the people began obeying the Word of the Lord. Having built the walls, now they wanted to build up their lives.

God wants us to help people repair their lives the way Nehemiah repaired the walls of Jerusalem. We should obey Him with joy because, as we read in Nehemiah 8:10, "The joy of the Lord is your strength."

PRAYER:

Dear Lord, I am so blessed to know that in everything I do, You are there to help me be strong and successful.

ESTHER

CHAPTERS
10

AUTHOR:
UNKNOWN

KEY VERSE:

"Yet who knows whether you have come to the kingdom for such a time as this?"
Esther 4:14

(Page 545 in the *Airship Genesis* Kids Study Bible)

AIRSHIP GENESIS

LEGENDARY BIBLE ADVENTURE

Esther was an amazing woman. In today's world, she could have been a movie star, a national leader, or the head of a business. But she lived long ago in the days of the Persian Empire. She became Queen of Persia.

This book tells how wicked Haman plotted to destroy Esther and her people, the Jews. It took all their courage, but Esther and her cousin Mordecai turned the tables on Haman, and the Jews were saved. This book tells how they did it.

Here's the odd thing about the book of Esther. This is the only book of the Bible that doesn't mention God. There's a reason. The writer wanted us to know that even when we don't see Him, God is at work. He causes everything to work together for His people.

Even when you don't know it, God is working on your behalf. He causes everything to work out for His people.

PRAYER:

Dear Lord, in the book of Esther I learned how You used one obedient person to protect Your people from harm; please help me to be courageous and willing to stand up for You today like Esther.

JOB

CHAPTERS
42

AUTHOR:
UNKNOWN

KEY VERSE:

"For I know that my Redeemer lives, and He shall stand at last on the earth." Job 19:25

(Page 566 in the *Airship Genesis* Kids Study Bible)

Do you worry about things? Everyone has problems, and sometimes we feel sad, worried, or lonely. That's how Job felt throughout much of this book. He was a rich man who lost everything except his faith in God.

In the first two chapters, the devil attacked Job. The devil thought Job would curse God, but Job blessed God instead. He said, "The Lord gave, and the Lord has taken away; blessed be the name of the Lord" (Job 1:21).

At the end of chapter 2, Job's friends visited him, and most of the book is about their discussions (Job 3–37). Finally God told Job to study the skies, the earth, the animals, and all the creation. The same God who made the universe is in charge of our lives (Job 38–41). In the final chapter, the Lord restored Job's possessions and blessed him for being faithful (Job 42).

Even when bad things happen, Job teaches us to say, "Blessed be the name of the Lord."

PRAYER:

Dear Lord, help me to remember that in every situation,
You are God and You alone are in charge of my life—I can
trust in Your loving care for me.

PSALMS

CHAPTERS
150

AUTHOR:
MANY

KEY VERSE:

"The Lord is my light and my salvation; whom shall I fear? The Lord is the strength of my life; of whom shall I be afraid?" Psalm 27:1

(Page 602 in the *Airship Genesis* Kids Study Bible)

God wants His creation to sing His praises. Listen to the birds tweet, the crickets chirp, and the dogs howl. He wants us to praise Him too, and that's what Psalms is about. A psalm is a sacred song. This book contains 150 of these songs, and they are full of emotion. Some are happy and others are sad. Some are even angry. But mostly they are full of praise.

Here are some fun facts about Psalms. It's in the middle of the Bible and has more chapters than any other book. It contains the longest chapter in the Bible (Psalm 119), and the shortest (Psalm 117).

King David wrote many of the Psalms, including the famous Twenty-Third Psalm. Millions of children have memorized it. You should too! It begins: "The Lord is my shepherd; I shall not want. He makes me to lie down in green pastures; He leads me beside the still waters."

When you read and memorize the Psalms, you feel like singing.

PRAYER:

Dear Lord, thank You for being my shepherd and guide; help me to trust in Your leading throughout my life.

PROVERBS

CHAPTERS
31

AUTHOR:
VARIOUS

KEY VERSE:

"Trust in the Lord with all your heart, and lean not on your own understanding." Proverbs 3:5

(Pages 686-687 in the *Airship Genesis* Kids Study Bible)

AIRSHIP GENESIS
LEGENDARY BIBLE ADVENTURE

Who is the smartest person alive? It's not the person with the highest IQ. It may not be a scientist, doctor, or professor. The smartest person is the one who knows how to live wisely. We become wise by reading and obeying the Bible—especially the book of Proverbs.

The word *proverb* refers to a wise saying, and the book of Proverbs is filled with them, like:

- "Trust in the Lord with all your heart, and lean not on your own understanding; in all your ways acknowledge Him, and He shall direct your paths."—Proverbs 3:5-6

- "A quick-tempered man acts foolishly."—Proverbs 14:17

- "Even a child is known by his deeds, whether what he does is pure and right."—Proverbs 20:11

A proverb is a heavenly rule for earthly living. The book of Proverbs is full of those. It has 31 chapters—one for each day of the month. To be wiser, read and heed the book of Proverbs.

PRAYER:

Dear God, help me to remember the words found in Proverbs— that I may learn how to trust in You, and know that "a good name is to be chosen rather than great riches."

ECCLESIASTES

CHAPTERS
12

AUTHOR:
KING SOLOMON

KEY VERSE:

"Remember now your Creator in the days of your youth." Ecclesiastes 12:1

(Page 727 in the *Airship Genesis* Kids Study Bible)

The word *Ecclesiastes* means "the preacher." That's how this book begins: "The words of the Preacher." We believe King Solomon was the preacher, and he wrote this book about the meaning of life.

Ecclesiastes begins by describing how empty we feel without the Lord: "Vanity of vanities, all is vanity" (Ecclesiastes 1:2). It ends by giving the solution: "Remember now your Creator in the days of your youth" (Ecclesiastes 12:1).

Many people don't know their purpose for being on earth. Even King Solomon struggled with that. One of the key words in Ecclesiastes is *vanity*, which means "emptiness." To Solomon, life without God is vanity. It doesn't matter how famous we are, how much money we have, or how much fun we find. Life is meaningless without God.

You have your whole life in front of you, so there's no need to wait. The best time to remember your Creator is now!

PRAYER:

Dear Lord, please grant me wisdom when I am young
to live my life for You—to keep Your commandments and
live fully for You throughout my life.

SONG OF SOLOMON

CHAPTERS
8

AUTHOR:
KING SOLOMON

KEY VERSE:

"Many waters cannot quench love, nor can the floods drown it." Song of Solomon 8:7

(Page 735 in the *Airship Genesis* Kids Study Bible)

Song of Solomon is a love song that describes the kind of love God wants to give a husband and wife for each other, and it reminds us of the kind of love God has for us.

These eight chapters tell how King Solomon fell in love with a woman called "the Shulamite." She didn't grow up in a palace. Yet somehow Solomon met her, and this book is his love song. It's a celebration of romance.

The first two chapters describe how Solomon and the Shulamite got to know each other. Chapters 3–4 describe their wedding. Chapters 5–7 show how they faced problems in their home. The end of the book, chapter 8, tells us they decided to keep on loving each other no matter what. The key verse says: "Many waters cannot quench love, nor can the floods drown it" (Song of Solomon 8:7).

When you love others, you want the best for them. Song of Solomon reminds us to love our families always, for that's how God loves us. He never quits.

PRAYER:

Father, please help me to be more like You—to love others with a pure heart, as You love me.

ISAIAH

CHAPTERS
66

AUTHOR:
ISAIAH

KEY VERSE:

"For unto us a Child is born, unto us a Son is given; and the government will be upon His shoulder. And His name will be called Wonderful, Counselor, Mighty God, Everlasting Father, Prince of Peace." Isaiah 9:6

(Page 746 in the *Airship Genesis* Kids Study Bible)

One day a man named Isaiah had a vision of a fantastic heavenly throne. Special angels were flying around, crying, "Holy, holy, holy!" The ground trembled like an earthquake, and smoke filled the air. The Lord wanted someone to deliver His message, and Isaiah said: "Here am I! Send me" (Isaiah 6:8).

In this way, Isaiah became God's prophet, and this book is a record of what God told him to say.

Chapters 1–35 were especially for the nation of Judah in the days of the Assyrian Empire.

Chapters 36–39 describe the Assyrian invasion and tell us how God sent a powerful angel to protect His people.

Chapters 40–66 were written to encourage people in the future, who would endure the Babylonian invasion.

Isaiah is full of predictions about the coming of Jesus Christ. Check out Isaiah 53, for example. Whenever we read that chapter—or any chapter in Isaiah—it makes us want to say as Isaiah did: "Here am I! Send me."

PRAYER:

Dear Father, this book reminds me that hundreds of years before the birth of Christ, the plan to send Him to earth to save us was announced. Help me share that wonderful plan of salvation with others.

JEREMIAH

CHAPTERS
52

AUTHOR:
JEREMIAH

KEY VERSE:

"Call to Me, and I will answer you, and show you great and mighty things, which you do not know." Jeremiah 33:3

(Page 850 in the *Airship Genesis* Kids Study Bible)

The Lord told Jeremiah, "Before I formed you in the womb I knew you; before you were born ... I ordained you a prophet to the nations" (Jeremiah 1:5). Jeremiah thought he was too young to do what God wanted. But the Lord helped him, and Jeremiah became a great prophet.

Jeremiah wrote down his sermons. He often told us what happened *before* he preached, what he said *as* he preached it, and what happened *afterward*. For example, in chapters 19–20, the Lord told Jeremiah to buy a jar from the local potter and smash it during his sermon. Jeremiah did so. His listeners didn't like what he said and had him beaten.

Sometimes we call Jeremiah the "Weeping Prophet." He lived in terrible times and watched his nation go from bad to worse. But he stayed faithful because he knew God had a plan.

Don't think you're too young to make a difference. The Lord has always had a plan for your life—even before you were born.

PRAYER:

Dear Lord, I am so grateful that You have a plan for me—a plan to give me "a future and a hope."

LAMENTATIONS

CHAPTERS
5

AUTHOR:
JEREMIAH

KEY VERSE:

"Through the Lord's mercies we are not consumed, because His compassions fail not. They are new every morning; great is Your faithfulness." Lamentations 3:22–23

(Page 883 in the *Airship Genesis* Kids Study Bible)

Did you know that sometimes even happy people cry? The prophet Jeremiah wrote Lamentations through tears. The word *lamentation* means "a song of sadness." Jeremiah wrote these sad songs after Jerusalem was destroyed in the Babylon invasion. The people had sinned against the Lord, and sin brings sorrow. Jeremiah, gripped with sadness, wrote the opening line: "How lonely sits the city that was full of people!" (Lamentations 1:1) That sets the tone for the book.

There are five chapters in Lamentations, and each one has 22 verses—except for chapter 3, which has 66 verses. Chapter 3 isn't just longer; it's happier. Jeremiah remembered something that made him feel better: "This I recall to my mind, therefore I have hope. Through the Lord's mercies we are not consumed, because His compassions fail not. They are new every morning; great is Your faithfulness" (Lamentations 3:21–23).

Whenever you feel sad, remember God's faithfulness. We can keep hope in our hearts. His blessings are new every morning.

PRAYER:

Dear God, thank You for being with me through every day and every situation I face in my life. Please give me patience to wait for Your timing.

EZEKIEL

CHAPTERS
48

AUTHOR:
EZEKIEL

KEY VERSE:

"I will put My Spirit within you and cause you to walk in My statutes, and you will keep My judgments and do them." Ezekiel 36:27

(Page 927 in the *Airship Genesis* Kids Study Bible)

Disappointment is how we feel when we lose a game, when a trip is canceled, or when we don't make the team.

That's how Ezekiel felt as he began writing his book. He had trained for priestly service in Jerusalem. But just as he became old enough to work in the temple, Babylonian soldiers seized him. They took him to a refugee camp far away. There alongside a river, the heavens opened and Ezekiel saw the glory of God (see Ezekiel 1).

For the rest of his life, Ezekiel cared for the displaced people streaming into Babylon from Judah. The first 24 chapters of Ezekiel tell us what he told the refugees *before* the final destruction of Judah. Chapters 25–32 were written *during* the siege of Jerusalem. The last part of the book, chapters 33–48, describes what occurred *after* the fall of Jerusalem and what will happen in the future.

Whenever you feel disappointed, tell God about it and trust Him. He has a way of turning disappointments into blessings.

PRAYER:

Dear Lord, please allow me to help someone today—to be an answer to their need in Your Name.

DANIEL

CHAPTERS
12

AUTHOR:
DANIEL

KEY VERSE:

"Daniel answered and said: 'Blessed be the name of God forever and ever, for wisdom and might are His. And He changes the times and the seasons; He removes kings and raises up kings; He gives wisdom to the wise and knowledge to those who have understanding.'" Daniel 2:20-21

(Page 946 in the *Airship Genesis* Kids Study Bible).

AIRSHIP GENESIS

LEGENDARY BIBLE ADVENTURE

Daniel is a favorite book of many people. In Daniel you meet hungry lions, towering statues, fiery furnaces, brave heroes, dazzling angels, frightening beasts—and, in the middle of it all, Daniel and his friends.

Like Ezekiel, Daniel was a young man kidnapped by Babylonian soldiers. He and his friends were taken to the godless city of Babylon to train for royal service. Babylon was a dangerous place, but Daniel made up his mind to remain true to God. The Lord gave him the ability to interpret dreams. That helped him become a powerful person in Babylon.

The first six chapters of this book describe Daniel's adventures, and the main lesson is, "The Most High [God] rules in the kingdom of men" (Daniel 4:17). The last six chapters are full of prophecies about the future. Here you'll find predictions about the first and second comings of Jesus to earth.

As you read this book, think about how God uses people like Daniel—and you—when we make up our minds to serve Him, even when few others do.

PRAYER:

Dear Father, may I always look to the future with confidence
as I remember that the "Most High" rules!

HOSEA

CHAPTERS
14

AUTHOR:
HOSEA

KEY VERSE:

"O Israel, return to the Lord your God, for you have stumbled because of your iniquity."
Hosea 14:1

(Page 976 in the *Airship Genesis* Kids Study Bible)

AIRSHIP GENESIS

LEGENDARY BIBLE ADVENTURE

You probably know the difference between Major League and Minor League teams. The Kansas City Royals are a Major League Baseball team. The Omaha Storm Chasers are in the Minor Leagues.

The last part of the Old Testament contains the writings of the prophets. The first three are Major Prophets because their books are longer—Isaiah, Jeremiah, and Ezekiel. The remaining prophets' books are shorter. We call these the Minor Prophets. There are twelve Minor Prophets between Hosea and Malachi.

Hosea was a Minor Prophet who married a woman named Gomer. She was not faithful to him, but Hosea loved her anyway. He told people that his marriage was a lesson about how God loved the nation of Judah. The people were not faithful to God, but He loved them anyway and was willing to bless them if they would seek His forgiveness.

Hosea is a Minor Prophet with a major message: "It is time to seek the Lord, till He comes and rains righteousness on you" (Hosea 10:12). Even when we fail to serve God faithfully, He is always faithful in His love to us.

PRAYER:

Dear God, thank You for loving me even when I make mistakes and fail to keep Your ways. You are faithful even when I am not.

JOEL

CHAPTERS
3

AUTHOR:
JOEL

KEY VERSE:

"Return to the Lord your God, for He is gracious and merciful, slow to anger, and of great kindness; and He relents from doing harm." Joel 2:13

(Page 980 in the *Airship Genesis* Kids Study Bible)

AIRSHIP GENESIS

LEGENDARY BIBLE ADVENTURE

Grasshoppers are odd insects with bent legs, big eyes, and long antennae. A locust is a large grasshopper. In some nations, swarms of locusts fly in like fleets of helicopters. They make the sky dark. They can destroy all the crops.

The prophet Joel preached during a locust invasion. He warned people to turn back to God. The locusts, he said, were a warning of judgment. The locust plague was a preview of the future when judgment will fall on those who reject God. This future time of judgment is called the "day of the Lord." See if you can find that phrase five times in this book.

Joel also described the wonderful things God has planned for His people in the future. The key verse is Joel 2:13: "Return to the Lord your God, for He is gracious and merciful, slow to anger, and of great kindness."

There's a great day coming. When we belong to the Lord we can look forward to it with excitement. The future doesn't belong to the locusts, but to the Lord.

PRAYER:

Dear God, I rejoice that You are gracious and merciful to me.

AMOS

CHAPTERS
9

**AUTHOR:
AMOS**

KEY VERSE:

"Seek good and not evil, that you may live; so the Lord God of hosts will be with you as you have spoken." Amos 5:14

(Page 988 in the *Airship Genesis* Kids Study Bible)

I magine flying over a farm. Down below is a fig orchard. Nearby are flocks of sheep. Taking care of it all is a hardworking farmer.

That's the kind of man Amos was. He wasn't a trained prophet but a farmer (Amos 7:14). He had no training in public speaking. Yet God sent him to preach the Word of the Lord in the nation of Israel.

Amos has nine chapters. The first two describe how God will judge the nations for their wickedness. Chapters 3–6 explain God's judgment on the nation of Israel because of the evil there. Chapters 7–9 contain promises of God's blessings on Israel in the future.

Perhaps you'll become a missionary. Perhaps you'll be a farmer, business leader, schoolteacher, banker, coach, or homemaker. Whatever God calls you to do, remember we all have a message from God for the world. Like Amos, we must share His Word boldly.

PRAYER:

Lord, help me love others as You love them,
unconditionally and full of grace.

OBADIAH

CHAPTERS
1

AUTHOR: OBADIAH

KEY VERSE:

"For the day of the Lord upon all the nations is near; as you have done, it shall be done to you."
Obadiah 1:15

(Page 995 in the *Airship Genesis* Kids Study Bible)

The name *Obadiah* means "servant of the Lord." There are about twelve men with this name in the Bible, and we don't know much about *this* Obadiah. But we know he wrote the shortest book in the Old Testament, and we know what his book is about. It's a warning to Edom.

The nation of Edom began with a man named Esau. You can read about him in the book of Genesis. He and Jacob were twin brothers, but their descendants didn't get along well. When the Babylonians destroyed Judah, the people of Edom rejoiced. They were glad when something bad happened to their neighbor. But Obadiah said they were wrong to rejoice, for the same fate awaited them. The Babylonians would destroy them too.

Proverbs 24:17 says, "Do not rejoice when your enemy falls, and do not let your heart be glad when he stumbles." Obadiah warns us against gloating when other people have problems. When we love people, we want the best for them. When we want God's blessings on others, we are like Obadiah—servants of the Lord.

PRAYER:

Dear Heavenly Father, give me a love for others so that
I rejoice when they succeed, not when they fail.

JONAH

CHAPTERS
4

AUTHOR:
JONAH

KEY VERSE:

"I cried out to the Lord because of my affliction, and He answered me." Jonah 2:2

(Page 998 in the *Airship Genesis* Kids Study Bible)

AIRSHIP GENESIS

LEGENDARY BIBLE ADVENTURE

The book of Jonah tells how God helped Jonah become a better person and a better prophet, and you'll enjoy reading every word. The first two chapters explain how God sent him to preach in Nineveh, the capital city of his enemy. Jonah sailed in the opposite direction. When a storm arose, he was thrown overboard. God sent a great fish to swallow him, and Jonah repented in the belly of the fish.

When the fish spit him out, Jonah traveled to Nineveh, but he still didn't have a good attitude. The last two chapters describe his anger when people repented. He didn't want God to spare them. He sulked under a vine. When God let a worm destroy the vine, Jonah was furious. The Lord showed him he was wrong to be more upset about a vine than about a city needing hope.

Did a fish really swallow Jonah? Genesis 1:1 says, "In the beginning God." If we believe those words, it's not hard to believe in miracles. Our God is able to do whatever He pleases, even with whales, worms, and storms at sea.

PRAYER:

Dear Lord, when I am weak, please help me to be strong.

MICAH

CHAPTERS
7

AUTHOR:
MICAH

KEY VERSE:

"He has shown you, O man, what is good; and what does the Lord require of you but to do justly, to love mercy, and to walk humbly with your God?" Micah 6:8

(Page 1006 in the *Airship Genesis* Kids Study Bible)

AIRSHIP GENESIS

LEGENDARY BIBLE ADVENTURE

Do you live in a big city or a small town? The prophet Isaiah lived in a big city and wrote a big book. The prophet Micah wrote a smaller book, and he was concerned about the small towns of Judah. Try reading through this book and circling all the names of the small towns mentioned. One was Bethlehem, and Micah predicted that's where Jesus would be born: "But you, Bethlehem Ephrathah, though you are little among the thousands of Judah, yet out of you shall come forth to Me the One to be Ruler in Israel" (Micah 5:2).

To God, there are no small towns, small churches, or small people. Everyone is important. He can use small things as well as big things. He can bless quiet people as much as loud people. He can use unknown people as much as well-known people.

The important thing is obeying Him. Micah 6:8 says: "He has shown you ... what is good; and what does the Lord require of you but to do justly, to love mercy, and to walk humbly with your God?"

PRAYER:

Dear Lord, please teach me Your ways
so that I may walk in Your paths.

NAHUM

CHAPTERS
3

**AUTHOR:
NAHUM**

KEY VERSE:

"The Lord is good, a stronghold in the day of trouble; and He knows those who trust in Him."
Nahum 1:7

(Page 1010 in the *Airship Genesis* Kids Study Bible)

The book of Jonah tells how the people of Nineveh repented when Jonah warned them of judgment. But a hundred years later, Nineveh was as bad as ever. This time God sent a message through the prophet Nahum.

Nahum has three chapters. Chapter 1 tells us *what* God will do to Nineveh—He will punish the evildoers. Chapter 2 explains *how* He will do it: "I will burn your chariots in smoke" (Nahum 2:13). The last chapter tells *why* God will judge Nineveh—because the city was filled with lies and robbery (Nahum 3:1).

This isn't just a message for Nineveh. It's for the whole world. God isn't going to let evil continue forever. The prophet Nahum tells of a coming day when God will correct all that is wrong with our world.

As you read this book, look for verses that encourage God's people. For example, Nahum 1:7 is a wonderful verse to learn: "The Lord is good, a stronghold in the day of trouble; and He knows those who trust in Him."

PRAYER:

Thank You, God, that You are my refuge in times of trouble.

HABAKKUK

CHAPTERS
3

AUTHOR:
HABAKKUK

KEY VERSE:

"The Lord God is my strength; He will make my feet like deer's feet, and He will make me walk on my high hills." Habakkuk 3:19

(Page 1017 in the *Airship Genesis* Kids Study Bible)

AIRSHIP GENESIS
LEGENDARY BIBLE ADVENTURE

Have you been upset recently? Is anything troubling you? When Habakkuk wrote his book, he was troubled too. But he knew what to do—he prayed about his troubles.

Habakkuk began with the words, "O Lord, how long ...?" He wanted to know how long God would put up with violence (Habakkuk 1:1–4). The Lord told him things would go from bad to worse (Habakkuk 1:5–11). Habakkuk asked why (Habakkuk 1:12–2:1). The Lord told him to walk by faith, and He reassured him that one day the earth would be filled with the knowledge of the Lord as the waters cover the sea (Habakkuk 2:2–20).

That encouraged Habakkuk. The last chapter is a song Habakkuk wrote, and the final verse says, "The Lord God is my strength; He will make my feet like deer's feet, and He will make me walk on my high hills" (Habakkuk 3:19).

When you're upset, read Habakkuk and think about its message: "The just shall live by his faith" (Habakkuk 2:4).

PRAYER:

Dear God, help me to read Your Word and remember
that my walk with You is by faith.

ZEPHANIAH

CHAPTERS
3

AUTHOR:
ZEPHANIAH

KEY VERSE:

"The Lord your God in your midst, the Mighty One, will save; He will rejoice over you with gladness, He will quiet you with His love, He will rejoice over you with singing." Zephaniah 3:17

(Page 1022 in the *Airship Genesis* Kids Study Bible)

What if you could predict what will happen tomorrow? We can't tell the future, but sometimes God revealed the future to His prophets in the Bible. When you read Zephaniah, you'll learn exciting things about days to come.

Read these quotes from Zephaniah and see if you can figure out what this book is about: "The day of the Lord is at hand .... The day of the Lord's sacrifice .... On that day .... The great day of the Lord is near; it is near and hastens quickly .... That day is a day of wrath, a day of trouble ... a day of clouds ... a day of trumpet .... In that day you shall not be shamed."

Like Joel, Zephaniah's message is about the Day of the Lord—that great day when Jesus will return to earth. On that day, He will do away with evil and make things right. On that day, He will bless His people and take care of us forever.

We can't tell the future, but we can tell what's going to happen in the future whenever we study these three chapters of Zephaniah.

PRAYER:

Dear Lord, I know the future is in Your hands. Help me
to trust fully in You and Your faithfulness.

HAGGAI

CHAPTERS
2

AUTHOR:
HAGGAI

KEY VERSE:

"'Be strong, all you people of the land,' says the Lord, 'and work; for I am with you,' says the Lord of hosts." Haggai 2:4

(Page 1024 in the *Airship Genesis* Kids Study Bible)

Never give up! That's the message of Haggai. This is a short book made up of several sermons (notice how Haggai dates each one). And it has an interesting background. According to Ezra 4:24–5:2, when the Babylonians destroyed Jerusalem they burned down the Lord's temple. Years later some Jews returned from exile to rebuild it. Their enemies bullied them and the workers became discouraged. They gave up on the project, and for several years nothing happened.

Finally two prophets showed up—Haggai and Zechariah. They encouraged the people to start over. Soon the city heard the sounds of construction from the temple site as one stone was laid upon another. The house of the Lord was rebuilt.

Haggai teaches us to never give up on anything God calls us to do. The key verse is Haggai 2:4: "'Be strong, all you people of the land,' says the Lord, 'and work; for I am with you.'"

Don't get discouraged. As you work for the Lord, remember He is with you.

PRAYER:

Father, give me the strength to do all
that You have planned for me.

ZECHARIAH

CHAPTERS
14

AUTHOR:
ZECHARIAH

KEY VERSE:

"Thus says the Lord of hosts: 'Behold, I will save My people from the land of the east and from the land of the west; I will bring them back, and they shall dwell in the midst of Jerusalem. They shall be My people and I will be their God, in truth and righteousness.'" Zechariah 8:7–8

(Page 1032 in the *Airship Genesis* Kids Study Bible)

Of course you can do it!

Sometimes we need encouragement like that. And that's a good way of explaining what Zechariah and Haggai told the Jews in Jerusalem who had stopped rebuilding the temple. In the book of Ezra, we learn how some of the Jewish people returned to Jerusalem from exile in Babylon. They wanted to rebuild the temple, but they grew discouraged. Haggai and Zechariah told them they could do it, for God was with them.

Zechariah has fourteen thrilling chapters about angels who ride horses (Zechariah 1:8-10), a man being attacked by the devil (Zechariah 3:1-7), a flying scroll (Zechariah 5:1-4), and a woman flying through the air in a basket (Zechariah 5:5-11). You'll also read a description of the last great battle in world history (Zechariah 12–14).

Zechariah is an exciting book with one great message: Keep working at whatever God gives you because He has a plan for the world, and He has a plan for you.

Of course you can do it!

PRAYER:

Dear God, thank You for the plans You have
for me and for the world.

MALACHI

CHAPTERS
4

AUTHOR:
MALACHI

KEY VERSE:

"'Bring all the tithes into the storehouse, that there may be food in My house, and try Me now in this,' says the Lord of hosts." Malachi 3:10

(Page 1043 in the *Airship Genesis* Kids Study Bible)

Do you sometimes argue with your dad or mom or teacher? In Malachi, the people of Judah argued with God. As you study this book, you'll see it's written like a conversation in which God's people argue with Him.

The Lord said, "I have loved you." But they said, "How?" The Lord said, "You have despised My Name." But they said, "Us?" The Lord said, "You have worn Me out." But they said, "How have we done that?" The Lord said, "You have robbed Me." But the people said, "What do You mean?"

Malachi lived about a hundred years after Haggai and Zechariah. The temple was again standing in Jerusalem and the Jews were back in Jerusalem. But their love had again grown cold. When Malachi tried to correct them, they argued. The Lord answered their arguments and helped them live for Him more faithfully.

When someone tries to correct you—especially a parent or teacher—don't argue. Listen to them and learn. That's the lesson of Malachi.

PRAYER:

Dear Lord, thank you for being faithful in every situation and teaching me how to live a blessed life.

▶ ▶ ▶ ▶ ▶ ▶ ▶ **BOOKS OF THE**

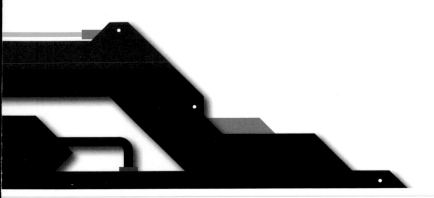

NEW TESTAMENT

MATTHEW

AUTHOR:
MATTHEW

CHAPTERS
28

KEY VERSE:

"Let your light so shine before men, that they may see your good works and glorify your Father in heaven." Matthew 5:16

(Page 1054 in the *Airship Genesis* Kids Study Bible)

Welcome to the world of Jesus! Matthew is the first of four Gospels. The word *Gospel* means "Good News."

Matthew 1:1 begins: "The book of the genealogy of Jesus Christ, the Son of David, the Son of Abraham." *Genealogy* refers to a family history, and Matthew gives us Christ's family tree. Then he describes the birth of Jesus, the visit of the wise men, and the early days of our Lord's work (Matthew 1–4).

Chapters 5–7 record the Sermon on the Mount. Here you'll find the Lord's Prayer and the Golden Rule. The rest of Matthew is a collection of sermons and stories relating to Jesus. Matthew often paused to explain how Jesus fulfilled Old Testament predictions about Him.

Read about the death of Jesus in chapter 27 and His Resurrection in chapter 28. The book ends with Jesus' words: "Go therefore and make disciples of all the nations" (Matthew 28:19).

As you read Matthew, you'll get to know Jesus and His Good News for you.

PRAYER:

Dear God, I pray that my life points people to Jesus
and His mission to redeem the lost.

BOOK: 41/66

MARK

CHAPTERS
16

AUTHOR:
MARK

KEY VERSE:

"For even the Son of Man did not come to be served, but to serve, and to give His life a ransom for many." Mark 10:45

(Page 1112 in the *Airship Genesis* Kids Study Bible)

Meet Mark. He was a teenager during the ministry of Christ. His mother had a large home in Jerusalem, and it became a meeting place for early Christians (Acts 12:12). When Paul left on his first missionary trip, Mark went along. But along the way, Mark turned back (Acts 13:13). Some people thought Mark was a failure, but Mark knew he wasn't a quitter. He went on to become the writer of the second Gospel.

Mark's story of the life of Christ is the shortest of the Gospels, and he wrote as if in a hurry. It's not that Mark wanted to rush the job. He was just excited to tell the story. He often used the word *immediately* to describe the action. See if you can find that word eight times in chapter 1.

Mark's excitement kept him going. He shows us there's a difference between being a failure and being a quitter. It's all right to fail, because that means we're trying. The secret is not quitting—and we never quit when we're excited about Jesus.

PRAYER:

Dear God, help me be a faithful witness for You—as I share the Good News of the Gospel with those around me.

LUKE

CHAPTERS
24

AUTHOR:
LUKE

KEY VERSE:

"For the Son of Man has come to seek and to save that which was lost." Luke 19:10

(Page 1159 in the *Airship Genesis* Kids Study Bible)

Luke was a doctor who loved Jesus. When he learned some people had written untrue stories about Christ, he decided to write a true account. He addressed his Gospel to a man named Theophilus. He began by saying something like this: "Dear Theophilus. Since many people are writing stories about Jesus, I thought I'd provide a correct account. I want you to know the true facts about Him" (see Luke 1:1-4).

That's how we got the Gospel of Luke.

Luke is the longest book in the New Testament, and it gives the fullest story of Jesus. Luke tells how Jesus was born in Bethlehem and laid in a manger. He describes what happened to Jesus when He was twelve years old (Luke 2:41–52). He tells us what Jesus said and did during His ministry. And Luke gives us the fullest account of what happened the day Jesus rose from the dead (Luke 24).

Luke gives us strong facts so we'll have a strong faith.

PRAYER:

Lord, thank You for saving me and redeeming my soul.

JOHN

CHAPTERS
21

AUTHOR: JOHN

KEY VERSE:

"Jesus said to him, 'I am the way, the truth, and the life. No one comes to the Father except through Me.'" John 14:6

(Page 1196 in the *Airship Genesis* Kids Study Bible)

Do you have a best friend? The apostle John thought of Jesus as his best friend. He called himself "the disciple whom [Jesus] loved" (John 19:26). The love of Jesus made John feel special. He wanted to share this love with others, so he wrote the fourth Gospel.

Here is the message of John: Jesus is more than a man. He is God Himself!

In John 1:1, John said about Jesus: "In the beginning was the Word … and the Word was God."

In John 20:28, Thomas said about Jesus: "My Lord and my God!"

The most famous verse in this Gospel is John 3:16, which sums everything up: "For God so loved the world that He gave His only begotten Son, that whoever believes in Him should not perish but have everlasting life."

The most important thing to know about Jesus is that He is both God and man, and it is through Him alone that we are saved from our sins. He loves us and wants to give us everlasting life. He wants to be our best friend forever.

PRAYER:

Dear God, thank You for sending Your Son,
Jesus Christ, to die for my sins.

ACTS

CHAPTERS
28

AUTHOR: LUKE

KEY VERSE:

"You shall receive power when the Holy Spirit has come upon you; and you shall be witnesses to Me in Jerusalem, and in all Judea and Samaria, and to the end of the earth." Acts 1:8

(Page 1208 in the *Airship Genesis* Kids Study Bible)

AIRSHIP GENESIS

LEGENDARY BIBLE ADVENTURE

You're going to love Acts. It lives up to its name—it's full of ACTion. This book tells how the Holy Spirit came from heaven to help Christians. You'll see how Peter escaped prison and how Paul escaped a sinking ship. Most of all, you'll see the boldness of the Early Church in telling others about Jesus.

The key verse is Acts 1:8, when Jesus said: "You shall receive power when the Holy Spirit has come upon you; and you shall be witnesses to Me in Jerusalem, and in all Judea and Samaria, and to the end of the earth."

Chapters 1–7 tell how the message of Jesus filled Jerusalem. Chapters 8–12 describe how the Gospel spread through Judea and Samaria. And chapters 13–28 tell how the Gospel reached the ends of the earth.

God gave us the Holy Spirit to help us share His message with others. He wants us to be people of action.

PRAYER:

Lord, give me the power to put my faith into action
and share the Gospel with the world.

ROMANS

CHAPTERS
16

**AUTHOR:
PAUL**

KEY VERSE:

"For the wages of sin is death, but the gift of God is eternal life in Christ Jesus our Lord." Romans 6:23

(Page 1258 in the *Airship Genesis* Kids Study Bible)

It's fun to learn big words. *Refrigerator* has five syllables. So does *imagination*. And *cafeteria*. Well, here's a Bible word with five syllables: *Justification*. It means that when we receive Jesus as Savior, God looks at us differently. He no longer sees our sins. He sees the goodness of Christ. When we are justified, it's just as though we had never sinned. We are friends with God and have everlasting life.

That's what Romans is about. The apostle Paul wrote to the Christians in Rome to tell them: "Therefore, having been justified by faith, we have peace with God through our Lord Jesus Christ" (Romans 5:1).

Romans has two parts. Chapters 1–11 explain how justification works. We have all sinned, but Jesus died and rose again for us to give us the gift of eternal life.

Chapters 12–16 tell us how justification changes the way we live. We should love others, respect our leaders, and stand up for what is right.

Romans is a book worth studying. And *justification* is a word worth knowing.

PRAYER:

Father, I am so grateful that nothing can separate me from Your love.

1 CORINTHIANS

CHAPTERS
16

AUTHOR:
PAUL

KEY VERSES:

"Love suffers long and is kind; love does not envy; love does not parade itself, is not puffed up; does not behave rudely, does not seek its own, is not provoked, thinks no evil; does not rejoice in iniquity, but rejoices in the truth; bears all things, believes all things, hopes all things, endures all things." 1 Corinthians 13:4-7

(Page 1281 in the *Airship Genesis* Kids Study Bible)

Have you ever argued with a friend? Quarreling upsets us, doesn't it? When we get into fights, we don't feel good about others. We don't feel good about ourselves.

In the ancient city of Corinth, there was a church of people who squabbled all the time. These people often got into arguments. The apostle Paul wrote two letters to them in the Bible. In this first letter, he had a lot to say about the problems they were causing.

Chapters 1–4 warn about bickering. Chapters 5–6 encourage us to be pure and good. Chapter 7 talks about marriage. Chapters 8–10 discuss what to do when we disagree over certain things. Chapters 11–14 have to do with worship practices. Chapter 15 is about the Resurrection. Paul ends with some personal advice in chapter 16.

One of the chapters of 1 Corinthians is especially wonderful. Chapter 13 is the Love Chapter of the Bible. Many people memorize its thirteen verses, because it gives us patience when we feel like arguing.

PRAYER:

Dear God, please give me the *agape* love that never fails.

2 CORINTHIANS

CHAPTERS
13

AUTHOR:
PAUL

KEY VERSE:

"For the weapons of our warfare are not carnal but mighty in God for pulling down strongholds."
2 Corinthians 10:4

(Page 1293 in the *Airship Genesis* Kids Study Bible)

What should you do when someone lies about you? To see what Paul did, read 2 Corinthians. He wrote this book because people were saying unkind things about him. Paul loved these people. He had started their church. Yet some had defamed him.

Paul defended himself in 2 Corinthians. He really wasn't too worried about what people thought of him, but he was concerned about what they thought of Christ. Since he was Christ's ambassador (2 Corinthians 5:20), he defended himself for Christ's sake.

In chapters 1–7, Paul answered those who criticized him. In chapters 10–13, he explained his background and his sufferings for the Gospel.

In the middle of the book—chapters 8 and 9—there's a wonderful passage about giving money to the Lord's work. Do you get an allowance or earn money? Put some of it in the offering at church, "for God loves a cheerful giver" (2 Corinthians 9:7).

The book of 2 Corinthians is really all about giving—giving answers to those who attack us, and giving money to the Lord who blesses us.

PRAYER:

Dear Lord, help me to trust in You even when I am
being attacked for my faith, and to show forgiveness
to those who falsely accuse me.

GALATIANS

CHAPTERS
6

**AUTHOR:
PAUL**

KEY VERSE:

"But the fruit of the Spirit is love, joy, peace, longsuffering, kindness, goodness, faithfulness, gentleness, self-control. Against such there is no law." Galatians 5:22-23

(Pages 1300-1301 in the *Airship Genesis* Kids Study Bible)

Strap on your backpack for a hike in the hills of Galatia. In Acts 13 and 14, the apostle Paul traveled through this region, preaching the Gospel. He told people that Jesus is God's only way of salvation. Paul was able to start several churches on his trip. But afterward, false teachers showed up. They said, "Jesus is *not* enough. You also have to become a Jew and keep all the Jewish habits and holidays."

When Paul heard this, he was distressed. He wrote a letter to these churches and told them: "I marvel that you are turning away so soon from Him who called you .... Even if we, or an angel from heaven, preach any other gospel to you than what we have preached to you, let him be accursed" (Galatians 1:6-8).

There are six chapters in Galatians. The first two tell us the Gospel is from God. The middle two tell us what the Gospel means. The last two chapters tell us why it matters. Studying Galatians is like hiking through the great truths taught by the apostle Paul.

PRAYER:

Dear Lord, help me display the fruit of the Spirit in my life so that others see You reflected in me.

EPHESIANS

CHAPTERS
6

AUTHOR:
PAUL

KEY VERSE:

"Put on the whole armor of God, that you may be able to stand against the wiles of the devil." Ephesians 6:11

(Page 1309 in the *Airship Genesis* Kids Study Bible)

Ephesians is about a rich person—you! If you're a Christ-follower, you're rich in happiness. You're rich in what God has for you in the future. Notice how Paul opened his letter to the Christians in Ephesus: "Blessed be the God and Father of our Lord Jesus Christ, who has blessed us with every spiritual blessing in the heavenly places in Christ" (Ephesians 1:3).

There are some special words to find in Ephesians. In chapters 1–2, look for the words *seated* and *sit*. God raised Christ from the dead and seated Him at His right hand in heaven. In a sense, when we belong to Christ, we are seated with Him (Ephesians 1:20; 2:6).

In chapters 4–5, look for the word *walk*. Walk worthy of Christ, walk in love, walk in light, and walk wisely (Ephesians 4:1; 5:2, 8, 15).

The word *stand* is important at the end of the book. We're to stand against the devil (Ephesians 6:11, 13, 14).

Sit. Walk. Stand. If you can remember those words, you'll know what Ephesians is about—and you'll be rich in Christ.

PRAYER:

Dear Heavenly Father, please help me walk in love and in Your peace, and to show Your light to others by my walk of faith.

PHILIPPIANS

CHAPTERS
4

AUTHOR:
PAUL

KEY VERSE:

"I can do all things through Christ who strengthens me." Philippians 4:13

(Page 1316 in the *Airship Genesis* Kids Study Bible)

Are you happy? We can't always be happy, but we can always keep joy in our hearts. That's what Paul told the church in the city of Philippi.

Acts 16 explains how this church was started. Paul and Silas entered Philippi and preached the Gospel. They were arrested, beaten, and thrown into prison. As they sang praises to God, an earthquake shook the building and set them free. Paul stayed and preached the Gospel, and several people became Christians. They started a church.

Years later, Paul was chained in another prison—in Rome. That's when he wrote the church in Philippi and told them, "Rejoice in the Lord always. Again I will say, rejoice!" (Philippians 4:4)

There are only four chapters in Philippians, but they are full of joy. Paul loved the Philippians very much. He didn't want them to worry about him. He wanted them to have the joy of the Lord in their hearts.

In the same way, the Lord wants you to have His joy today. He wants you to rejoice in the Lord always. And I will say it again: Rejoice!

PRAYER:

Dear Father, thank You for giving me the peace and joy
that only comes from knowing You!

COLOSSIANS

CHAPTERS
4

AUTHOR:
PAUL

KEY VERSE:

"As you therefore have received Christ Jesus the Lord, so walk in Him, rooted and built up in Him and established in the faith, as you have been taught, abounding in it with thanksgiving."
Colossians 2:6-7

(Page 1319 in the *Airship Genesis* Kids Study Bible)

AIRSHIP GENESIS
LEGENDARY BIBLE ADVENTURE

If we don't understand who Christ is, we won't be able to serve Him as we should.

That's the central message of Colossians.

Here's the background. A man named Epaphras shared the Good News about Jesus with his hometown of Colosse. A church started there, and Epaphras prayed for the church earnestly (Colossians 1:9; 4:12). When false teachers came to town, Epaphras was upset. These teachers said untrue things about Jesus.

Epaphras visited the apostle Paul to talk about the problem, and Paul wrote to the church to correct their view of Christ. Paul's main point was: Jesus is "the image of the invisible God ... All things were created through Him and for Him. And He is before all things" (Colossians 1:15–17).

There are four chapters in this book. The first two emphasize the identity of Jesus. The last two tell us how to please Him.

When someone asks what your life is all about, you can answer with one word—Christ! In all things, He must be in first place (see Colossians 1:18).

PRAYER:

Dear Lord, thank You for this book, which reminds me that I need to keep You first in my life.

1 THESSALONIANS

CHAPTERS
5

AUTHOR: PAUL

KEY VERSE:

"For the Lord Himself will descend from heaven with a shout, with the voice of an archangel, and with the trumpet of God. And the dead in Christ will rise first." 1 Thessalonians 4:16

(Page 1325 in the *Airship Genesis* Kids Study Bible)

AIRSHIP GENESIS

LEGENDARY BIBLE ADVENTURE

I f you packed a suitcase and traveled to the nation of Greece, you could spend the night in a city called Thessaloniki. It's the second largest city in Greece. It was an important city in Bible times too. The apostle Paul started a church there (Acts 17:1-6). His enemies drove him out of town before he could tell the new church everything they wanted to know about the return of Christ to earth.

That's why Paul wrote two letters to them—1 Thessalonians and 2 Thessalonians. Both explain the Second Coming of Christ. Notice how every chapter in 1 Thessalonians ends with a reference to Jesus' return to earth.

It's fun to travel. But the most exciting trip in history is the one we'll take when Jesus comes for us. We'll be "caught up" into the clouds "to meet the Lord in the air. And thus we shall always be with the Lord" (1 Thessalonians 4:17).

PRAYER:

Dear Lord, even though I do not know the day when You will return, help me to pray and live in expectation of that day.

2 THESSALONIANS

CHAPTERS
3

**AUTHOR:
PAUL**

KEY VERSE:

"But as for you, brethren, do not grow weary in doing good." 2 Thessalonians 3:13

(Page 1329 in the *Airship Genesis* Kids Study Bible)

Anticipation means "looking forward to something"—being excited about the future. Maybe you're anticipating a ball game, a birthday party, or a trip.

The Thessalonians were anticipating the return of Christ. They were suffering persecution and could hardly wait for the Lord to come back for them. Paul wrote 2 Thessalonians to help them better understand the Lord's return.

In chapter 1, Paul said that when Jesus comes again, He will punish evildoers and be glorified in us, His people.

In chapter 2, he explained how a "man of sin" would arise before the return of Christ and take control of the world. But Jesus will consume him "with the breath of His mouth and destroy with the brightness of His coming" (2 Thessalonians 2:8).

In chapter 3, Paul told us to stay busy while we await the Lord's return. Don't be lazy. Don't grow tired of doing good things (2 Thessalonians 3:13).

Every day we should look forward to the Second Coming of Christ. But we must not forget to *work* for Him while we *wait* for Him.

PRAYER:

Dear God, as I look for Christ's return, help me to stay busy working for You as I wait for that coming day.

1 TIMOTHY

CHAPTERS
6

AUTHOR:
PAUL

KEY VERSE:

"Let no one despise your youth, but be an example to the believers in word, in conduct, in love, in spirit, in faith, in purity." 1 Timothy 4:12

(Page 1334 in the *Airship Genesis* Kids Study Bible)

It's a good idea to go to church every week. There we sing, pray, and worship the Lord. We study the Bible at church. We serve the Lord and care for each other there.

But how does a church work? In 1 Timothy, Paul wrote to his friend Timothy, a leader in the church of Ephesus. An important verse in this book is 1 Timothy 3:15: "I write so that you may know how you ought to conduct yourself in the house of God, which is the church."

- Chapter 1 tells us what should be taught at church.

- Chapter 2 explains how to pray at church.

- Chapter 3 describes who should lead the church.

- Chapter 4 tells the pastor what to do.

- Chapter 5 helps us care for groups in the church.

- Chapter 6 explains why we should give money to support the work of the church.

It's a privilege to go to church. It's wonderful to know how we should conduct ourselves in the house of God.

PRAYER:

Thank You, dear Lord, for the opportunity to go
to church and to learn more about You.

2 TIMOTHY

CHAPTERS
4

**AUTHOR:
PAUL**

KEY VERSE:

"All Scripture is given by inspiration of God, and is profitable for doctrine, for reproof, for correction, for instruction in righteousness." 2 Timothy 3:16

(Page 1339 in the *Airship Genesis* Kids Study Bible)

Who's your hero? Everyone needs someone to admire. Timothy's hero was the apostle Paul. According to Acts 16, Timothy was a youth when Paul led him to Christ. Timothy traveled with Paul and became one of his greatest workers.

When we read 2 Timothy, we're reading Paul's final letter, and it's to Timothy. Paul wrote it from prison in Rome. Soon he would be put to death by order of Emperor Nero. Time was short, and Paul still had things to tell his son in the faith.

You can read those words in 2 Timothy, where you'll hear the old apostle say things like: "Timothy ... Stir up the gift of God which is in you .... Do not be ashamed of the testimony of our Lord .... Be strong in the grace that is in Christ Jesus .... Continue in the things which you have learned .... Preach the Word!"

We all need a hero like Paul. Ask God to give you the right heroes. And remember—if you live for Christ today, one day you'll be a hero to others.

PRAYER:

Dear God, I want to be a person who finishes the race well—please help me stay strong in my faith in Christ Jesus.

TITUS

CHAPTERS 3

AUTHOR: PAUL

KEY VERSE:

"For the grace of God that brings salvation has appeared to all men." Titus 2:11

(Page 1343 in the *Airship Genesis* Kids Study Bible)

AIRSHIP GENESIS

LEGENDARY BIBLE ADVENTURE

Crete is a beautiful island in the Mediterranean Sea. It has high mountains, lots of beaches, and good weather. You can visit there whenever you read the book of Titus.

Titus was a Christian leader who moved to Crete to strengthen the churches. The apostle Paul told him: "I left you in Crete, that you should set in order the things that are lacking, and appoint elders in every city as I commanded you" (Titus 1:5).

As you read this letter, notice that one of the main subjects is self-control. The people of Crete were not self-controlled. They were "liars, evil beasts, lazy gluttons" (Titus 1:12). Throughout this letter, we're told to be self-controlled. That means we don't do everything we want, because some things aren't right. We do some things we don't want to do, because doing them is right. When we're self-controlled, we resist temptation and we live as we should even when we don't feel like it.

That's what Paul wanted Titus to teach the islanders of Crete. And that's what the Lord wants to teach us too.

PRAYER:

Father, help me to resist temptation by
keeping the Bible as my guide.

PHILEMON

CHAPTERS
1

AUTHOR:
PAUL

KEY VERSE:

"If then you count me as a partner, receive him as you would me. But if he has wronged you or owes anything, put that on my account." Philemon 1:17-18

(Page 1346 in the *Airship Genesis* Kids Study Bible)

Near the town of Colosse lived a wealthy man named Philemon. He owned a slave named Onesimus. In those days, some of the new Christians didn't yet realize slavery was wrong.

One day Onesimus ran away. In Rome he met the apostle Paul, who told him about Jesus. Onesimus became a Christ-follower, and he felt he should return to Philemon. But that was dangerous because runaway slaves were beaten or killed.

Paul wrote a letter for Onesimus to take to Philemon—and that's the little letter you'll read in Philemon. We can only imagine how Philemon felt when he saw his runaway slave and read this letter. Paul told Philemon to treat Onesimus like a brother. "If he has wronged you or owes anything, put that on my account," he said.

This is a short letter—only 25 verses—but it shows us we should treat people with love and respect. We should treat them like our own family. We should treat them with the love God has shown us.

PRAYER:

Dear Lord, help me to show love, to forgive, and to respect others because of the love You have shown to me.

HEBREWS

CHAPTERS
13

**AUTHOR:
UNKNOWN**

KEY VERSE:

"Now faith is the substance of things hoped for, the evidence of things not seen."
Hebrews 11:1

(Page 1355 in the *Airship Genesis* Kids Study Bible)

Back in Genesis, God chose a man named Abraham to start a special nation. Sometimes we call this nation Israel. Sometimes we say they are Jews. Another name for them is Hebrews. Jesus was a Hebrew. After Jesus rose from the dead, some of these Hebrews became His followers. Because of that, they suffered for their faith. But it hardly mattered to them, because they were so excited about Jesus.

Many years passed, and one day they faced another period of suffering. This time some of them wondered if they should keep following Christ. The writer of Hebrews—we don't know who he was—told them to never give up (see Hebrews 10:32-36).

The book of Hebrews tells us we should never give up on Jesus because He is greater than anyone (Hebrews 1:1–10:18), and living for Him is greater than anything (Hebrews 10:19–13:25). That's the message of this book.

Whatever happens, said the author, we should "run with endurance the race that is set before us, looking unto Jesus" (Hebrews 12:1-2).

PRAYER:

Lord, give me strength and wisdom to be
a champion of faith for You!

JAMES

CHAPTERS
5

AUTHOR:
JAMES

KEY VERSE:

"If any of you lacks wisdom, let him ask of God, who gives to all liberally and without reproach, and it will be given to him." James 1:5

(Page 1362 in the *Airship Genesis* Kids Study Bible)

We have a book of wise sayings in the Old Testament called Proverbs. In the New Testament, we have another book of wise sayings called James. It's named for the man who wrote it. James was the half-brother of Jesus. James wasn't a follower of Christ until after Jesus rose from the dead. But when he *did* decide to be a Christian, he did so with all his heart. He became very wise, and his book is full of "wisdom that is from above" (James 3:17).

Anytime you need good advice, read James. He tells you what to do in trouble (James 1:2), when tempted (James 1:12), and when angry (James 1:19-20). He shows us how to treat people who are poor (James 2:2-5). James has lots to say about the way we speak with our tongues (James 3:1-12). He explains why we get into fights (James 4:1-6), and he tells us how to resist the devil (James 4:7-8). He ends his book by giving us some good advice about praying (James 5:13-18).

Whenever you read and heed James, you become wiser.

PRAYER:

Jesus, I ask for Your wisdom throughout my life. Teach me Your ways and help me to follow them with my whole heart.

1 PETER

CHAPTERS 5

AUTHOR: PETER

KEY VERSE:

"Casting all your care upon Him, for He cares for you." 1 Peter 5:7

(Page 1371 in the *Airship Genesis* Kids Study Bible)

AIRSHIP GENESIS

LEGENDARY BIBLE ADVENTURE

If you like to fish, you'll like Peter. He was a fisherman. He had a large boat on the Sea of Galilee and used large nets to catch fish. He sold his fish all across Israel, and this provided income for his family. One day Jesus came to his village and said, "Follow Me." Peter left his boats to become a disciple of Jesus. After Jesus rose from the grave, Peter became a leader in the Church. He traveled everywhere preaching the Gospel. He became a fisher of men (Mark 1:17).

One day Peter felt he should write a letter to encourage Christians who were suffering. Many people were suffering persecution. Some had been thrown in prison. Others had been insulted and bullied. Some had been beaten. Peter knew it wasn't always easy to stand up for Christ, so he wrote a book to strengthen us.

As you read 1 Peter, see if you can find this key sentence: "For to this you were called, because Christ also suffered for us, leaving us an example, that you should follow His steps" (2:21).

PRAYER:

Father, help me to honor You, even through
suffering—for Jesus suffered for me.

2 PETER

CHAPTERS
3

AUTHOR:
PETER

KEY VERSE:

"The Lord is not slack concerning His promise, as some count slackness, but is longsuffering toward us, not willing that any should perish but that all should come to repentance." 2 Peter 3:9

(Page 1374 in the *Airship Genesis* Kids Study Bible)

Do you have trouble remembering to brush your teeth? To do your chores? Or finish your homework? Sometimes we need people to remind us.

That's what Peter did in 2 Peter. He said, "I will … remind you always of these things …. I think it is right … to stir you up by reminding you" (2 Peter 1:12–13).

Peter wrote this letter from prison. He was near the end of his life, but he was able to write a final letter to remind us of his teachings. In the first chapter he reminds us of the core beliefs that come from Scripture. In the second, he warns us against false teachers. In the last chapter, he tells us what will happen when Jesus comes again. This is a very exciting passage, for it explains how the earth will be destroyed by fire one day. "Nevertheless we, according to His promise, look for new heavens and a new earth" (2 Peter 3:13).

Even at the end of his life, Peter was reminding us to look forward.

PRAYER:

Dear Father, help me not to forget Your Word.
Remind me to live for You every day.

1 JOHN

CHAPTERS
5

AUTHOR: JOHN

KEY VERSE:

"If we confess our sins, He is faithful and just to forgive us our sins and to cleanse us from all unrighteousness." 1 John 1:9

(Page 1377 in the *Airship Genesis* Kids Study Bible)

The apostle John wrote the Gospel of John. He also wrote three short letters, which we call 1 John, 2 John, and 3 John. We believe he lived to be very old. We're glad he lived long enough to write the book of 1 John, because it's full of words like *love* and *life* and *light*. John was concerned that we love each other. He wanted us to know that Jesus loves us enough to give us eternal life. He told us to walk in the light.

A very important verse is near the end of the book—1 John 5:13: "These things I have written to you who believe in the name of the Son of God, that you may know that you have eternal life."

When you become a Christ-follower, you can know for sure you have eternal life. If someone asks you, "Are you going to live forever in heaven?" you don't have to say, "Maybe." You can say, "Yes!"

Because of Jesus, you have *love* and *life* and *light*.

PRAYER:

Dear God, thank You for the gift of eternal life through Jesus Christ.

2 JOHN

CHAPTERS
1

**AUTHOR:
JOHN**

KEY VERSE:

"This is love, that we walk according to His commandments. This is the commandment, that as you have heard from the beginning, you should walk in it." 2 John 1:6

(Page 1384 in the *Airship Genesis* Kids Study Bible)

It's fun to learn a secret code. Let's say you want to write a letter to your friend, Abe. Just give each letter a number. A = 1. B = 2. C = 3. D = 4. E = 5. Using that code, your friend's name is 125.

Many people believe the apostle John used a secret code when writing 2 John. Because of persecution, he didn't want to reveal his location or the name of the church he was addressing. So he wrote his letter to "the elect lady and her children." He ended his letter saying, "The children of your elect sister greet you."

Many people believe the "elect lady" and "your elect sister" were code words for two churches, and the children were those who attended those churches.

But there was nothing coded about the central message of his letter. Verses 1-6 tell us to love each other. Verses 7-13 warn against those who lie and give wrong teachings.

Understanding the message of 2 John is as easy as 1, 2, 3.

PRAYER:

Dear Lord, please help me to stand for what is right.

3 JOHN

CHAPTERS
1

**AUTHOR:
JOHN**

KEY VERSE:

"Beloved, do not imitate what is evil, but what is good. He who does good is of God, but he who does evil has not seen God." 3 John 1:11

(Page 1386 in the *Airship Genesis* Kids Study Bible)

Here is the shortest book of the Bible—the third letter of the apostle John. You can read it quickly; but if you slow down enough to study it, you'll meet three interesting characters.

The first was Gaius. He's the man John addressed in this letter, and you can read about him in verses 1–8. John loved this man and thanked him for all he did for the Christians. Gaius was always eager to help godly teachers who traveled among the churches.

The second was Diotrephes. You can read about him in verses 9–11. He was proud and selfish. He hindered those who traveled from church to church. He wanted all the attention for himself.

The third man is Demetrius, and John wrote about him in verses 12–14. He had a good and respected testimony.

Which of these three are you most like? Are you like Gaius, eager to help? Or like Diotrephes, wanting attention? Or like Demetrius, respected by all?

PRAYER:

Dear Heavenly Father, help me be selfless and to put others first, so that I can show Christ's love to the world around me.

JUDE

CHAPTERS
1

AUTHOR:
JUDE

KEY VERSE:

"To God our Savior, who alone is wise, be glory and majesty, dominion and power, both now and forever. Amen." Jude 1:25

(Page 1389 in the *Airship Genesis* Kids Study Bible)

Two books of the Bible were written by men who had grown up with Jesus. They were James and Jude, the sons of Joseph and Mary. That makes their books special, for these men had known Jesus all their lives, even as children.

Jude's book is short but strong. In verse 3 it says: "Contend earnestly for the faith which was once for all delivered to the saints."

Jude was alarmed because false teachers were in the Church. He called them "clouds without water" and "autumn trees without fruit" (verse 12). Most of Jude is a warning to reject false teaching, but he ended his book on a note of praise: "Now to Him who is able to keep you from stumbling ... be glory and majesty ... both now and forever. Amen."

Whatever people say, we can trust the Bible. If we believe the wrong things, we'll live the wrong way. But God is able to build us up in the most holy faith (verse 20).

PRAYER:

Dear God, help me to stay fixed on the Truth You have taught me—especially when things go wrong around me—and help me to keep my trust in You.

REVELATION

CHAPTERS
22

AUTHOR:
JOHN

KEY VERSE:

"'I am the Alpha and the Omega, the Beginning and the End,' says the Lord, 'who is and who was and who is to come, the Almighty.'" Revelation 1:8

(Page 1391 in the *Airship Genesis* Kids Study Bible)

In Revelation you'll see a vision of Jesus on His throne. You'll read about the future battle for control of planet earth. You'll meet angels and demons and dictators and heroes. You'll learn how the world will end, and you'll get a sneak peek of our eternal home in heaven.

The apostle John wrote this book. He's the same man who wrote the Gospel of John and 1 John, 2 John, and 3 John. The theme of the book is found in the first verse: "The Revelation of Jesus Christ, which God gave Him to show His servants—things which must shortly take place."

Chapter 1 is an introduction to the whole book. Chapters 2–3 contain messages to seven churches John sent the book to. Chapters 4–18 reveal what will happen during the Great Tribulation, the period of time immediately before Jesus returns. Chapter 19 describes the Second Coming of Christ. You'll read about the final judgment in chapter 20. And chapters 21–22 describe our eternal home.

It is an exciting book to read!

PRAYER:

Dear God, as I wait for Christ's return, help me to
faithfully live in expectation of that day!

PLAN OF SALVATION

Are you ready to discover life's greatest gift by accepting Jesus as your Savior? **Today you can!**

ASK

BELIEVE

CONFESS

TRUST

PRAY

1

First, ASK Him to forgive you.

We are all sinners and need Jesus as our Savior.

For all have sinned and fall short of the glory of God.
Romans 3:23

2

Second, BELIEVE in Him.

Because God loves us, He sent His only Son to save us from our sins and offer life with Him in heaven.

For God so loved the world that he gave his one and only Son, that whoever believes in him shall not perish but have eternal life.
John 3:16, NIV

3

Third, **CONFESS** your sins.

Only a God who is sinless could save us from our sins. Jesus provided a way for us to be saved by coming to earth to die in our place.

To become a Christian, confess your sins and accept Jesus as your personal Savior—believing that He died for you and will guide you through life until you see Him in heaven one day.

But if we confess our sins, God will forgive us. We can trust God to do this. He always does what is right. He will make us clean from all the wrong things we have done.
1 John 1:9, ERV

4

Fourth, TRUST Him with your future.

One day when Christ returns, everyone who believes in Him will be taken to heaven to be with Him forever!

Romans 10:13 says, "Everyone who calls on the name of the Lord will be saved" (NIV).

The ... gift of God is eternal life through Christ Jesus our Lord.
Romans 6:23, NLT

5

Fifth, PRAY the sinner's prayer.

If you'd like to follow Jesus today, here's what you can pray:

Dear Jesus, thank You for dying on the cross in my place. I accept You as my Savior and invite You into my heart. Please forgive me for all my sins, and help me to follow You every day of my life.

I love You Lord, Amen!

AIRSHIP GENESIS
KIDS STUDY BIBLE

This Bible takes children on an exciting adventure through God's Word, providing real-life applications for children living in today's world. This complete Bible contains New King James Scripture with unique information throughout including Bible Heroes, Rupert Reports, Power Force articles, 100 Bible Blasts to memorize, 66 Mission Overviews, contemporary art featuring the Genesis Exploration Squad, and so much more.

It is available in two unique cover styles—Hardback and TechTile Leather.

For more information, go to **AirshipGenesis.com**.

MISSION QUEST

52 Learn It & Live It Faith-Building Missions

What is more important than for each of us to know about God and His Word? How do we learn it? By reading it and applying the lessons in practical ways.

Turning Point is pleased to present a unique 52-week devotional for children themed around a unique quest—a *Mission Quest*. The 52 topics were chosen specifically to help young people grow in their knowledge of God's Word and to learn how to apply those truths.

Each week features a Mission Quest (devotional), Mission Challenge (application), Mission Code (memory verse), and Mission Completed (sticker).

This weekly devotional will help build *out-of-this-world* kids! For more information, visit **AirshipGenesis.com.**

DAVID JEREMIAH

AIRSHIP GENESIS
LEGENDARY BIBLE ADVENTURE™

MISSION QUEST
KIDS DEVOTIONAL

MISSION 16:
THE SECRET TO WISE CHOICES

CHOICES

105

BLAST OFF!:

Incredible Readable Rhymables

Blast Off!: Incredible Readable Rhymables is a hardcover, colorful children's book that will take you on a delightful, yet meaningful, quest to discover answers to some of the biggest questions about the Bible, God, Jesus, the Holy Spirit, sin, forgiveness, and salvation—all in whimsical rhymes. The crew of the Genesis Exploration Squad hosts this amazing journey that leads boys and girls through an exhilarating Pathway to learn Bible truths.